Contents

Review

Background Reading

People in the story

Gail Klutesi
a nineteen-year-old college student and a Native Canadian from the Nuu-chah-nulth band

Grace Klutesi
Gail's mother, also a band member, and the leader of the protest at Big Tree Country

Bob Klutesi
Gail's father, also a band member, and a logging supervisor at Island Forest Products

Shane Barnett
a nineteen-year-old biology student and Gail's best friend

Ann Wong
a TV news journalist in her late twenties

Neddie Wakes
a manager at Island Forest Products and Bob Klutesi's boss

The story is set in a valley called Big Tree Country on an island on the west coast of Canada.

Chapter 1

The thin line

It was Monday morning and I stood at the end of the road, watching for the logging trucks to arrive. Although it was June, I had to stamp my feet to keep warm. My mother noticed how cold I looked, so she lent me her button blanket.

I loved that blanket and I tied it tightly around my shoulders. Like all our traditional button blankets, Mom's was made of pieces of black and red wool fabric, sewn together. What made it different was that my great-grandmother had stitched the shape of an eagle onto it and outlined the bird in pearl-white buttons. The sign of the eagle was like a family crest. Mom had been given the blanket by her mother. It had passed from mother to daughter for three generations.

Twenty-two of us—some from our tribe, as well as our friends and supporters from the town of Johnson Bay—formed a line blocking the logging road. That was the only way to save some of the oldest and tallest trees in the world. They grew in a valley that we called "Big Tree Country."

For thousands of years, we Nuu-chah-nulth have lived near that valley on a remote island off Canada's west coast. The valley had never been logged because it was so far from roads and from big cities. Two years ago, the government had sold the right to log Big Tree Country. The government had never asked us or anyone else about it when it made the deal with Island Forest Products. The company had promised to bring jobs to our community. Now Island

Forest Products was building a road to the valley, so that it could cut the forest down.

Today, we *had* to stop them. We had taken some boards and made a small traffic barrier. Several people held up signs saying "Save Big Tree Country," "Stop Logging," and "Make this Forest a Park."

A TV news crew had come from the city to record the protest. *That would help us,* I thought. The sun was shining on the forest valley. I could hear the birds singing in the trees. Maybe people watching the news would see what we were going to lose if this forest were cut down.

I twisted one of my braids nervously. When were the loggers going to come?

I looked over at Shane Barnett, one of the people from Johnson Bay helping to block the road. Some people think he's my boyfriend, but he's just my best friend. We went to the same high school, the only one in town, so now we hang out together at college.

"What do we do when the loggers get here?" I asked.

Shane must have seen how worried I looked. So he put away the smart phone he'd been checking. Then, as if he were a politician announcing something very important, he ran his hand through his wavy hair. He adjusted the funny-looking black glasses on his nose and he cleared his throat.

"We'll put up a big traffic sign that says 'Road closed.' That'll turn them back."

I groaned at the bad joke. "*If* they know how to read."

"You mean, like *books*?" he laughed.

Then I laughed, too, because he hasn't picked up a book in years. Shane's studying biology, but he likes to spend his time on computers. I never see him without a smart phone or a tablet computer in his hand. He always reads online.

I read books because I'm studying history. I've always been inspired by men and women who showed courage in dangerous times. I've always wondered whether I would be brave enough to be a heroine. Now here I was helping to block a logging road and save our forest.

Sure enough, even as we were talking, Shane pulled out his smart phone. He started doing something with it.

"Checking your fan mail?" I asked.

He pointed his phone at the line of protesters. "No, I'm taking a video. Then I'm going to post it."

"You'll let the world know about Big Tree Country? And we'll all become famous."

Shane nudged me with his elbow. "We won't have to wait that long. Look at that TV reporter talking to your mom."

The TV reporter must have been interviewing Mom because she'd organized the protest. I didn't encourage the reporter by looking in her direction, but she and her cameraman came over to us. She was an attractive Asian woman with permed shoulder-length hair. She looked like she was in her late twenties. She had on a jacket and she carried a large microphone.

"You're Gail Klutesi, aren't you?"

"Yes, can I help?" I asked.

She passed me a business card. "Ann Wong, *The Nightly News*. May I ask you a few questions? I've been following the Big Tree Country story for two months . . ."

Shane interrupted. "Two months! We've been fighting for this park for two years!"

Shane was right. It had been two years. That was when we learned that Island Forest Products had the right to log Big Tree Country.

That was when the company announced that it was going to build a road to it. But I gave Shane a dirty look. He shouldn't have been so critical. We needed to get Ms. Wong on our side.

I turned to her. "Big Tree Country has never been protected. It never had to be. Now the government has given permission to Island Forest Products to cut down the forest. The Nuu-chah-nulth people have lived here for a long, long time. We have always preserved this forest. There are plants and animals here that you can't find anywhere else."

Trying to keep his temper this time, Shane added, "We've got to get the government to make a park here."

Ms. Wong stepped in front of the camera, and they started filming. "Today, I'm here with a small band of protestors. They're taking on one of the biggest logging companies around, Island Forest Products. The company has the right to log these trees."

She turned to me and the camera followed. "But people like Gail Klutesi are fighting to save the forest. Three weeks ago, the government promised a decision on whether to make Big Tree Country a park. They still haven't decided."

Ms. Wong pushed her microphone toward me. "So, why do we need to save the forest, Gail?"

"Because it's a forest with big trees like that one." I pointed to a fir tree behind me which stood on a small ridge. It towered above the trees beside it. It must have been about forty meters tall.

"That fir tree is over a thousand years old. A thousand years old! That tree was growing before any Europeans set sail for Canada. In fact, it was growing when there was still a Roman empire."

Ms. Wong stared at the tree. "That's a big tree all right."

"We call it 'Magic,'" I said.

She smiled. "Magic? That's quite a name. How do you know it's a thousand years old?"

"We measured it on Saturday. I tried to put my arms around the tree. I couldn't reach more than a quarter of the way. Then Shane and I climbed it."

Ms. Wong was shocked. "You climbed that tree?"

"Well, Shane climbed the tree first, and he helped me up. I named the tree 'Magic.' It felt like magic to sit in a big tree like that."

Besides computers, Shane loves rock climbing, so he had brought his climbing harness and a rope to climb the biggest tree he could find. That turned out to be Magic. To get up it, he climbed up a much smaller tree growing beside Magic. From the smaller tree, he moved across to Magic and started climbing it. About twenty meters off the ground, Magic divides into three large branches. Shane stopped there and tied one end of his rope to the tree. Then he dropped the other end of the rope to me with his climbing harness, so that I could get up, too.

Ms. Wong shook her head in disbelief. "Look at the size of that tree."

Not only did we climb it, but there was something else. Shane and I had carried some boards up with us. We nailed them together to make ourselves a platform which we could sit on, a "tree sit." That way if the protest continued, we could even sleep in the tree. Shane and I even planned to try spending Monday night in the tree sit. But rather than tell Ms. Wong that information and get it broadcast on TV, I kept that part a secret.

"These big old trees are worth a lot of money," Shane explained. "That's why Island Forest Products is building a logging road here. Once they finish the road, it won't take them long to cut down the forest."

"But they replant the trees, don't they?" asked Ms. Wong.

"Sure, they replant," said Shane. "The government makes all of the logging companies do that. But the companies only let the new trees grow to be 40 or 50 years old. Then the companies cut them all down and replant trees again. The companies want to make money from the trees as soon as they can."

At that moment, we heard the Island Forest Products trucks driving along the road. Everyone turned to watch them. Six trucks drove up, including two very large ones with some heavy equipment for a big logging operation. Ms. Wong and her cameraman hurried down the road to film them.

As the trucks approached, the drivers honked their horns to get us out of their way. My mother signaled that no one should move from their positions. None of us did, so the loggers had to stop and park their trucks on the side of the road. The men started opening their doors and jumping out. They were wearing orange hardhats with "Island Forest Products" printed on them. Several loggers shouted and swore at us for blocking the road and wasting their time.

Mom walked down our line, encouraging everyone. "Don't worry. We're all in this together."

The morning grew warmer so I took off her button blanket and returned it to her. It passed from one generation to the next when a mother felt that her daughter had come of age. I hoped that one day soon she would pass it to me. Mom smiled, put the blanket over her shoulders, and moved further down the line.

At that moment, the supervisor of the loggers, a big heavy man with short, black hair and an orange hardhat, climbed out of a truck. He wore big logging boots and he carried a map under his arm. It was my father, Bob Klutesi.

Chapter 2

A family conflict

All morning, I had been dreading this moment. Apart from everything else, Mom and Dad had split up last year and they didn't get along very well.

A few loggers started to gather around my father. He waved them away with his rolled-up map. He tossed the map into his truck, then he headed toward our line. Then he walked over to me.

"Did you and your mother ever think about this?" He gestured at the forest. "I'm a logger. This is my job."

"Dad, you can't cut down these trees. They should be saved in a park," I said.

He sighed and crossed his arms. "*You* might want a park. But the people in Johnson Bay need jobs. And that's what Island Forest Products will give them."

"This is Nuu-chah-nulth land, Dad," I added. "We never gave it away. The government just took it. Then they gave it to Island Forest Products."

Dad shook his head. "Right now, our people need jobs more than land, Gail."

Shane cut into the conversation. "Mr. Klutesi, how long are your men going to be loggers? What are they going to do after they cut all the trees down?"

Dad looked annoyed. He had always liked talking with Shane when he came over to see me. That was before my parents had broken up and Dad had moved out. Now my father's expression suggested that he felt that Shane had betrayed him, too.

"Listen, even a few months' work would help some people. And after the trees are cut, people can go tree planting."

Shane shrugged. "Sure, you can all be tree planters for a while. What comes next? It's going to take years before the trees are big enough to cut down again."

I guess Dad couldn't think of a good reply. So, he criticized Shane instead. "It's easy for you to talk. Your family's never been poor."

Shane's face reddened. Everyone knew that his dad was a wealthy lawyer. People often held his father's money against him. They claimed that he was spoiled. They said that he had no sympathy for the poor in our town.

Angrily, I turned to my father. "That's not fair, Dad."

Mom heard us arguing and she hurried over. She's much smaller than Dad, but that didn't stop her from confronting him. She put her hands on her hips and asked, "How can you log this forest, Bob? You used to love big trees."

He sighed. "We've all got to work, Grace."

"What happened to the man I married?" she asked.

"There's nothing I can say, Grace. We disagree on everything now."

Mom shook her head. "Then forget about you and me. What about our people? The Nuu-chah-nulth have lived near this forest for thousands of years."

His eyes narrowed. "Times change. It's time our people did, too. I'm not going to quit logging just because we're in Big Tree Country."

"Dad, you can't do it. You've got to stop." I argued.

A tall, gray-haired man in his fifties, wearing a suit jacket and a tie with his orange hardhat, pushed through the noisy crowd of loggers and protestors that had begun gathering around my parents. The loggers and protestors were shouting at each other. But he ignored them and forced his way to the front of the crowd. He was the local manager of Island Forest Products, Dad's boss, Neddie Wakes.

"Why are you people trying to shut down a perfectly good business? Island Forest Products has been cutting down trees on the west coast for years."

Shane snapped, "That's why there're no old forests left."

"What about making a park here, Mr. Wakes?" I asked. "It's only one valley."

His face twisted in anger. "There'll never be a park here."

Then he noticed that our argument was being filmed by Ms. Wong and her cameraman. He quickly turned away. He motioned to the men in his crew to leave. "Let's get back to our trucks. I've called the police. Let them break up the protest."

Soon, two black police vans pulled up, and so did the old yellow bus from our high school. I couldn't figure out why the school bus was there, but the police vans meant that arrests were coming.

Ms. Wong and her cameraman filmed the policemen getting out of their vehicles. We all knew Officer Savard who worked in Johnson Bay. But there were six other policemen with him. Later, I learned that the extra men came from the city.

Officer Savard took a loudspeaker and addressed us. "We don't make the laws here. We just make sure they're obeyed. The company has the legal right to log this forest. We have an order from a judge to clear you from this road. That makes it a law. You've got ten minutes to leave. Otherwise, you'll be arrested."

That warning started the people on either side of me talking. No one wanted to go to jail. Two people quit the line. Ashamed, they avoided looking at the rest of us. As they walked down the road to their vehicles, the loggers called them names and laughed at them.

Officer Savard signaled and the policemen advanced to our line. He turned on the loudspeaker again. "You're each facing a $500 fine. Maybe jail time. That means a permanent police record. Do you people want that?"

The new threat scared people even more. Shane began arguing with someone who wanted to give up. A few others started looking around nervously. Were people going to give up so easily?

I would never dream of quitting. All it took was one look down the road. Trees had been cut down on either side of it. All that was left were tree stumps, rocks, and mud. Nothing would grow there for a long time.

"We want our forest," I shouted.

I couldn't believe I had dared to say that. But I felt angry. I closed the fingers of my hand into a fist, then I raised my fist into the air. "Save the trees. We want our forest."

People up and down the line repeated my words. "We want our forest."

Soon the whole crowd chanted. "Forest! Forest!"

Officer Savard cut off the chant with his loudspeaker. "Your time's up, people. We're going to start arresting you."

No one in the line moved. The policemen dragged five people away.

The rest of us sang to keep up our spirits. We started with a Nuu-chah-nulth war song. The words say "We are the people who stand our ground. We will not be moved." We sang an old American protest song, too, "We Shall Overcome Someday." That song came from the struggle for civil rights. Its message is that through our efforts, one day we will make a better world.

The policemen made two more arrests. Then Officer Savard and another man headed in my direction.

Mom stepped in their path. Officer Savard and the second policeman twisted her arms behind her back. They locked the handcuffs on her wrists. Her face showed a flash of pain.

That really upset me. "Go easy on Mom!"

Officer Savard snapped at me as he started pushing her in the direction of a police van. "We warned everyone to leave."

Mom tried to smile. "Don't worry, dear." She addressed the other protestors. "Keep the faith, everybody. Keep it peaceful. Don't give them an excuse to treat us roughly."

"That's enough out of you." The second policeman gave her a push.

Other policemen moved to arrest Uncle Joseph. As if he were following Mom's advice, he held out his arms for the handcuffs. Then he told us all something in our native language, so that the police couldn't understand him.

"They don't have enough space in their vans for all of us. We're going to win this fight."

Uncle Joseph was right. The police had already filled their vans with protestors. Even with just twelve of us left, we could still block the road. We all felt relieved.

Then the door of our old high school bus opened. A familiar, white-haired old man stepped out. It was Mac, the school bus driver. He ducked behind the yellow bus. That was where he went during the school term when he was on duty and didn't want to be seen smoking a cigarette.

Then I realized why Mac felt ashamed. Today, he worked for the police, not the school. The police began pushing handcuffed protestors onto his bus. They had more than enough space for the rest of us.

I turned to Shane. "Are you thinking what I am?"

He nodded. "Yeah, our 'Plan B.'"

Shane and I had talked about that plan. It was a desperate one. But it was the main reason why we'd built the tree sit on Magic.

We dashed from the line and ran toward the woods. That move surprised everyone. Other protestors broke from the line and ran, too. But they went in different directions. I didn't know if the police were chasing us or if they were running after someone else. At any moment, I expected someone to catch me.

Chapter 3

The runners

Shane and I crashed through the undergrowth as we ran into the forest. I could smell the fragrant scent of the fir tree needles, the leaves of the big trees. We rushed to Magic. The rope from the tree sit hung in front of us. I glanced behind us. The police had not come. Not yet. They were still chasing the other runners.

Our plan was to climb up Magic and stay in the tree sit. Safety laws require that loggers cutting down trees work at least two hundred meters away from people and buildings. Island Forest Products would have to make a wide circle around us to keep building the road and cutting down trees.

Shane seized the rope. Then he dropped it, looking panicked. "I forgot my climbing harness! I must have left it with my pack back on the road."

"What do you mean?" I asked.

"We can't climb the rope without a harness, Gail. It's got to be twenty meters to the tree sit. That's almost a six- or seven-story building. If we fall, we'll be killed."

"Then how are we going to save Magic?"

Desperately, Shane moved his hands rapidly up and down the tree trunk, searching for footholds. "I don't know."

We didn't have a lot of time. We couldn't go back for the harness. The police were surely going to turn up any moment.

Then he noticed something on the ground. With a shout, he picked it up. He showed me a coil of rope. "I left this on Saturday. I can make us a climbing harness."

I couldn't believe it. "Even if you could make one, Shane, we don't have much time. The police will be here any moment."

He waved me away. "I'm fast. Just look out for them."

I shook my head. Then I walked a few meters away. I could watch the road, but still keep an eye on Shane.

Shane put part of the rope around his waist and tied a loop in it. Then he laid the rest of the rope on the ground and quickly made it into a figure eight shape. He stepped into each loop of the figure eight. Then he pulled the figure eight up his legs. He tied together the loops around his legs to his waist.

"This is my climbing harness," he explained. "Now I'm going to attach it to the climbing rope on Magic."

Shane still had unused rope, so he took out his pocket knife and cut off two uneven lengths of it. He took the shorter piece, made it into a loop, and attached it to the rope harness around his waist. He took the longer piece and made a loop for his right foot. Then he made a special knot on both pieces and attached them to the climbing rope hanging from Magic.

He showed me the two knots. "These are called 'Prusik knots.' You need two of them to climb the tree. You stand up in the first one, the foot loop. That tightens the knot by your foot. It takes all your body weight. The second knot, the

one by your waist, is loose. So you slide the second knot up the climbing rope. You lean back. Almost like sitting down. The knot at your waist tightens up. Now it takes all your weight. So, you can loosen the first knot, and take your foot out of the loop. You move that first knot farther up the climbing rope. Then you step into it, getting higher on the climbing rope. You keep repeating the whole process."

"Have you ever climbed with these knots?" I asked.

He hesitated. "Not very much . . ."

"What does that mean?"

"You learn how to tie it in climbing school. I never use it because I always carry a regular harness." He loosened his knots. Then he stepped out of his rope harness. He passed it to me.

"Why are you giving it to me?" I asked.

"You're going first."

My mouth dropped with surprise. "Me? What do you mean?"

"If I go first, who's going to coach you if you get stuck? I might even have to climb part of the way up the tree to help you."

I handed the harness back to him." This isn't a very good plan, Shane."

"We've got to get up the tree. And there's no other way of getting both of us up."

I grabbed the harness. They had to move fast to avoid the police.

Shane lifted me onto his shoulders to help me start climbing. After a little coaching from him, I figured out how to pull myself up the rope using the two knots. I climbed four or five meters. Then I looked back at him.

He had his smart phone out. He was filming me.

"What are you doing?" I asked.

"This is amazing stuff, Gail. The scared expression on your face. You can see how hard it is to climb. I'm going to post it all over the Internet."

"That's just great," I replied. "Now the whole world's going to watch me lose my nerve."

Now that I knew I was on camera, I started picking up my speed. About halfway up Magic though, my nerve failed. Suddenly, I knew I was going to fall. I had climbed so high up. My harness didn't look very strong. Neither did the knots. My legs started trembling. The rope swayed. I didn't dare look down, but I called for help.

"Shane, I'm stuck!" I shouted.

Shane never replied. I called to him again. Nothing. Why wasn't he answering me? It would be just like him to be checking his smart phone or something. I called again. I didn't dare look down. That Shane! He's probably doing it to make me try harder. Again, I fought the urge to look down. If I did, I knew that I'd freeze completely.

So, I took a deep breath. I tried to focus on the tree trunk in front of me. I could break off little pieces of the red-brown bark under my fingers. In places around me, small branches with green needles had broken through the bark. There were even patches of bright green moss. The tree trunk was alive with different types of life.

I moved the knot up the rope. I started climbing again.

I startled a small gray-and-white bird with a long, black beak. The little bird quickly hid somewhere higher up in the tree. That excited me. I realized that the little bird was a marbled murrelet, rarely seen, because it only lives in old trees like Magic.

At last, I looked up. I saw the tree sit right above me. I reached up to the boards and I pulled myself up. Then I lay down on the tree sit, exhausted.

After a few minutes, I looked around. The tree sit was about the size of a double bed. We had placed it in the tree at the point where three big branches separated from the trunk. The branches formed a kind of cradle. The platform rested there. We had also tied the platform to the branches for extra safety. Then we had wound the rope around the branches to act as a fence, preventing anyone from falling off the tree sit. Finally, we had hung a blue plastic sheet over the tree sit to make it a little warmer at night and to protect us in case of rain.

I felt so tired. I just wanted to close my eyes and sleep there for a while. But I had to take off the harness and throw it to Shane. He needed it to climb up.

I leaned over the edge of the platform to call him. That was when I understood why he hadn't answered me before. He was trapped.

Chapter 4

Alone at the top

Shane stood near the base of the tree, caught between Officer Savard and a second policeman. They closed in. Shane tried to run away, but the second policeman ran at him from behind and knocked him down. Shane lay face down. The second policeman climbed over him, twisted his arms back and put handcuffs on him.

I quickly pulled up the climbing rope. No one was coming after me.

Officer Savard saw that and shouted, "Get down from there! You're breaking the law."

Shane had managed to get to his knees. He yelled to me, "Don't give up, Gail. You've stopped the loggers!"

The second policeman pushed Shane to the ground again. "Shut up! You're in enough trouble."

Officer Savard looked up at me. "If you stay in that tree after I've warned you, you're going to be in more trouble than your friend."

I yelled back. "We've tried everything else to save this forest. Nothing's worked."

Officer Savard shook his finger at me. "I'm warning you. You'd better get down."

Just then, I heard other voices in the forest. I looked over and saw my father and Mr. Wakes hurrying toward Magic. Ms. Wong and her cameraman followed at some distance.

As soon as he was close to Magic, Dad yelled, "What do you think you're doing, Gail? Get out of that tree."

"As long as I'm here, you won't be able to cut it down. You're not even going to get near."

"This is outrageous," Neddie Wakes complained. "We have a whole crew here today. We're going to have to send them home. Bob, get your daughter out of that tree."

"Did you hear that, Gail?" asked my father. "Because of you, some people might not even get paid today."

I shouted back at them. "I'm not letting you cut down this tree."

My father replied, "It's an old tree. It's going to fall anyway."

That comment made me mad. "Magic might grow for another hundred years. Maybe two hundred."

Shane managed to get partly back up. He was kneeling. "You're not talking about one tree. You want to cut down all of the trees."

"Shut him up," retorted Officer Savard.

The second policeman grabbed Shane by his shirt collar. "I'll take him to the van."

He began to drag Shane off. But Ms. Wong and her cameraman had started filming. They stood in his way.

"Any comments for us?" Ms. Wong asked the policeman.

He snapped at her, "We're just doing our job. This man was part of a group blocking a logging road. He tried to run away and we caught him. End of the story."

Shane piped in, "There's something wrong with the law."

"Let's get a move on." The policeman pushed Shane along.

Officer Savard turned to the reporter. "Ms. Wong, please. You're just encouraging these people."

"We're covering the news," she said indignantly. "It's our job."

Officer Savard waved her off. Then he turned to my father. "Your daughter's going to be in a lot of trouble if she doesn't get down from that tree. She was part of an illegal protest on the road. She ran away from us. Now I've ordered her to get down from the tree, but she won't leave. That's breaking the law again. She might have to go to jail."

"Gail, did you hear that?" asked my father. "You get down here!"

I was scared. But I couldn't let the forest be cut down. I shouted back, "I'm staying here."

My father sounded frustrated. "You're going to ruin your life. For what? A tree?"

I shook my head. "I'm trying to save a forest."

"What are you going to do, spend the night in that tree?" he asked.

"I'll spend a year here if I have to."

Dad threw up his arms in disbelief. "That's crazy! Gail, staying up there isn't going to stop us. We'll just rope off an area around your tree and cut down everything else."

Mr. Wakes snapped at him, "Don't tell her our plans."

"She's got to see how hopeless it is," replied my father. "Then she'll come down."

He turned to me again, his voice sounding desperate. "Gail, the company's going to lock down this whole valley. They're going to put a gate on the logging road to stop anyone but company men from getting up here. They're going to put security guards around this tree. Then they're going to wait until you're so hungry that you come down by yourself. Then they're going to take you to the police. So, why not give up now? The police will go easier on you."

Officer Savard waved me down. "That's right. If you come down now, we'll drop some charges against you."

Dad stood beside him, nodding in agreement, and waving me down, too.

My decision seemed very clear. I took a deep breath. "I'm going to stay here as long as I can. Even if you start cutting down other trees, I'm still slowing you down. And as long as I'm in Magic, I can save this tree."

Hearing that, Dad stood there shaking his head. It seemed like he didn't know what else to say.

Neddie Wakes stepped closer to the tree. "You should listen to your father. It's crazy to spend the night here."

I ignored Mr. Wakes. When he saw that, he tried a different approach.

"This is bear country," he began. "Every year they attack people. Have you thought of that, Gail?"

I couldn't believe it. Mr. Wakes was trying to scare me with bears! The black bears in this forest are as frightened of people as we are of them. Whenever Shane and I walked in the forest, we made noise to avoid surprising a bear and frightening it into charging at us. Whenever we went camping, we put the food outside our tent in a bag. Then we hung the bag from a tree branch, high enough to be out of reach for any bear. If bears become accustomed to eating people's food, even their garbage, they become dangerous.

Meanwhile, Ms. Wong's cameraman pointed his camera up at me, waving his hand to get my attention, so that he could film me. I waved back and moved to the edge of the tree sit where he could catch me on video. A girl in a big tree? That would definitely be in the news.

Ms. Wong stepped in front of the camera to deliver an update for *The Nightly News*. "Gail Klutesi, the only protestor to avoid arrest today, has climbed a thousand-year-old tree. Efforts to get her down are failing."

Her remarks on camera proved too much for Officer Savard. "All right, that's enough. This isn't a circus." He clapped his hands together. "Ms. Wong, you have to leave. You're interfering with police work."

"OK, sorry, we're leaving," replied Ms. Wong. She signaled to the cameraman. He put down his camera and they walked quickly away.

"We've got to get her down," insisted my father.

Mr. Wakes smiled. "Give me a chance."

Then he looked up at me, rubbing his hands together. "Tonight, you're going to be alone with the bears, Gail." He added in a scary voice. "A bear could tear you apart."

He was still trying to frighten me into leaving Magic. I felt like laughing at him. Clearly, he knew nothing of the Nuu-chah-nulth tribe or our stories. We feel as comfortable with bears as we do with the other animals in the forest. In fact, in our stories, bears are like people. Bears live in villages with wooden houses just as we do. And just like us, bears walk around their villages, talking, even arguing with each other.

Mr. Wakes went on. "You know, because bears have four legs, they can run a lot faster than people can. And they have sharp claws. It's easy for them to climb trees."

Not a tree this high, I thought to myself. All this talk about bears reminded me of one of our most famous stories, "The Bear Mother." In it, people and bears become related. A girl makes fun of a family of bears and they kidnap her and take her to their village. After a few months, she falls in love with a handsome young bear and they marry. The couple has children. Although the kids look like bears, the bears in the village reject them because they're part human. Those bears must have been worried they'd become related to people like Neddie Wakes.

I was tired of listening to him. "Mr. Wakes, I'm not afraid of bears. Some days I like animals a lot more than I like people. Especially people trying to scare me."

Wakes threw up his hands in frustration. "I hope a bear climbs that tree and eats you."

"Hey, that's my daughter you're talking to," my father protested.

Officer Savard raised his hand to stop them. "That's enough out of you two. This isn't working. We've got a busload of people to take to the police station. Just leave her in the tree."

So Officer Savard, my father, and Mr. Wakes left the forest. At last, I had some peace.

I did have a big problem though. Unlike a possible bear attack, it was a very serious one. And it was immediate. I didn't have any supplies. I had climbed Magic with a little pack. It had a water bottle and two chocolate bars in it. Just thinking of that water bottle made me thirsty. So, I took it out of my pack and drank a mouthful. What a relief! Then I looked at the bottle and realized that I had much less than I thought. I had heard that you could go four or five days without water. I hoped I wouldn't have to test that.

Now I wasn't thirsty, but I felt hungry. I didn't want to think about it, either. So, I broke off a piece of chocolate and ate it. The chocolate tasted delicious. But it made me thirsty again. I had to save my water. So, all I could do was to lick my lips.

I would have taken out my smart phone and called Shane. He might have had some ideas. But of course, he had been arrested, and so had my mother. So, I did what I could. I held my phone at arm's length and took a few photos of me sitting in Magic. Then I posted them on Facebook with a message:

"Help me stop the logging in Big Tree Country. I don't have much food and water. Look for my tree sit, high in Magic, the big fir tree in the forest at the end of the logging road."

My friends would read it. Some of them had promised to help block the road. They'd never shown up. But all I needed was one person to bring me supplies.

The sun began to set, and the forest grew larger, and quieter. The idea of sleeping in a tree now felt strange and frightening. I sat so high off the ground. Was the platform solid? I ran my hands over the boards. They seemed to be nailed together well enough. But would they take my weight? Carefully, I shifted around on the boards. I listened to see if I heard any of them creaking. Not a sound. They appeared to be solid.

I was going to be sleeping on them, so I thought I'd better make myself comfortable. I took off my shoes and put them under my little pack, making a sort of pillow for my head. Then I laid down.

The platform seemed very small. I reached out with my arms and touched the edges of it. That was all the space I had. The rope that we had run back and forth between the branches to fence in the platform had a small gap for climbing up and down. It was possible that I could roll right off the platform and fall out of the tree. I put on my harness and tied myself to a tree branch. To make sure, I laid flat on my back, too.

I remembered that I had a plastic sheet in my bag. We had used it for sitting on. I took it out, covered my head with it, and wrapped the rest of it around my body. That helped a little.

So, I lay there, trying to keep warm. As for sleep, I doubted it would prove possible. I didn't think I could relax while worrying about rolling off the platform. It was going to be a long night.

At that moment, I heard a strange sound. I quickly sat up. It took me a few seconds to realize that I was hearing the flapping of giant wings. A big bird was landing in the highest part of the tree. There was still light. I could see dark wings and a head covered in white feathers. That big bird had a wingspan almost two meters wide. It was a bald eagle. I had read somewhere that eagles often nest in the tops of old growth trees. It must have had a nest in Magic. Now I really felt like I was living in another world.

Chapter 5

Surrounded

The sunlight filtering through the branches of the tree woke me on Tuesday morning. My whole body ached from sleeping on wooden boards. I had a splitting headache from my lack of water. I could hear my stomach grumbling.

Reaching for my water bottle, I took a swallow. Now the bottle looked half empty. I examined it carefully. I couldn't have already had that much. Then my stomach started making noises again. I felt very hungry!

I ate a big piece of chocolate. Then I felt thirsty again. Then I felt hungry after I took a tiny sip of water. How much longer could I carry on like this?

To distract myself, I checked my Facebook post on my phone. Had anyone read it? To my surprise, I found 350 comments. A lot of people had watched the story about the logging road blockade and my escape to Magic on *The Nightly News*. I could hardly believe it. Friends urged me to fight on. Strangers from all over the world offered to help.

Help—that's what I needed! But to get to me, someone would have to sneak past the gate on the road. Then it would take them a long time to hike to my part of the forest. After that, they still had to find Magic. It seemed impossible.

I looked over the messages quickly. Then I noticed my phone battery flashing. Not only was I short of food and water, and warm clothes, but I didn't have a spare phone battery. I turned off my phone and set it down.

I racked my brains trying to think of something I could do. I remembered that a stream ran near the road. I wondered if I should get down from Magic and try to find it. At least that way, I would have some water.

I looked out of my tree sit. To my surprise, I saw several figures entering the forest. My heart leaped. Some people were coming to help.

Then I saw that they were all wearing red jackets. The jackets had lettering that read "Security." They must be the security men that my father had mentioned.

One of the men came to the foot of Magic. He was no ordinary security guard. It was Neddie Wakes.

"I thought the bears had got you," he shouted, laughing at me. "So, are you ready to quit now?"

It shocked me to see him. He had planned it that way, too. He had pretended to be a security guard by wearing one of their jackets. I didn't want him to know that he had caught me by surprise. Worse still, he might realize that I was desperately low on supplies.

I yelled back at him. "Not at all. I've got free rent up here. The view's very good, too."

That remark made him mad.

"You're not going to enjoy the view very long," he retorted. "We've got tents set up here. We're going to stay here until we starve you out of that tree."

I could imagine that day pretty clearly: my cheeks looking hollow; the teeth in my mouth feeling loose; my lips cracked and dry from lack of water.

But I pretended that I wasn't worried. "Good. I think I need to lose a little weight."

"Is that right?" Mr. Wakes took a paper bag out of his jacket pocket and opened it up. "I was planning on saving this chicken sandwich for lunch. But I'm feeling a little hungry now."

That sandwich sounded delicious. I could imagine sinking my teeth into it.

He ate a bite, then waved his sandwich at me. "There's another half in the bag. You come down now and I'll share it with you—half this sandwich. The best offer you'll get. And another thing, we're going to start logging the trees in Big Tree Country. It was a little bit of trouble going around you, but we've roped off your area now. You'll be hearing from us soon. You'll be hearing trees fall."

"I've saved this part of the forest," I answered.

Mr. Wakes finished off his sandwich, then he crumpled up the bag and threw it to the ground. "You've saved it for now. But how long can you live without food and water? And when you come down, we're cutting this big old tree down. Then we're taking you to the police."

Then he walked away. The two other men in red jackets came to the tree. They walked around Magic, studying it from various angles. I guessed that they would be my regular guards.

One of them called to me, "Hey, stupid, give up. And save us a lot of trouble."

I couldn't think of anything to say. I was barely hanging on. I had never felt so hungry. All I had eaten was some chocolate and a light breakfast on Monday morning. And I desperately needed water. I laid down on the tree sit. I felt weak. I thought I should save my strength. I drifted off to sleep.

A buzzing chainsaw woke me up. It seemed too close. Dangerously close. I looked out and saw a logger cutting into a huge tree only thirty or forty meters away.

He was breaking the rules. He was cutting a tree much too close to me. If that tree fell in my direction, it would crash into Magic. That would knock me right out of the tree. Or it would knock Magic down and take me with it. Even if I had wanted to leave Magic, it would be more dangerous on the ground now. So, I stayed where I was.

I listened carefully. The sawing lasted almost half an hour. Then I heard a loud crack. The tree broke into two pieces. The upper part tipped over. Its branches collided with those of a tree nearby and it fell with a roar of cracking branches. I closed my eyes, praying that it would miss Magic.

The tree hit the ground with a loud boom. It had missed me. The loggers cheered. And a tree that was nearly as old as Magic was gone forever. I heard some flapping of wings. I looked up and saw the eagle that had been nesting in Magic fly away.

Everything in the forest went quiet for a while. Any animals nearby must have been terrified. Then I heard a chainsaw cutting into a new tree, and a second chainsaw starting on another tree. The sounds of chainsaws and of trees falling tortured me. They were logging the trees in Big Tree Country and they were cutting them so close that I was in danger.

That was how Tuesday passed. One tree cut down after another. I felt terrible. There was nothing I could do to stop it.

By sunset, when the logging finally ended, I felt completely drained of emotion. I was exhausted. I had been worrying about getting hit by a falling tree. And I was powerless to save those trees.

Above all, I felt so hungry and thirsty. I took a button from my shirt and sucked on it. I had heard of people dying of thirst who did that. It helped a little. I huddled on the platform, trying not to think of food. Thoughts of food came all the same. I thought of what I had eaten on Monday morning. Cereal with milk. Bread. An apple. Then I worked my way back, remembering a week of meals. Curried chicken. Salmon. A turkey sandwich.

That night I was too tired to worry about falling out of the tree. But I was too hungry and thirsty to sleep very well, either.

Wednesday morning, woken by the chainsaws, I had the last of my chocolate. And I drank most of my water. That was all I had to keep me going. I lay on the platform, too weak to try to figure out which trees were being cut down. I hardly even thought about Magic getting hit by one.

That afternoon, my father came by. He was the last person I wanted to see. More pressure to give up. I felt so mentally exhausted that I didn't think I could argue with him. It took all my strength just to sit up and listen. He shouted over the noise of the chainsaws, "Are you OK, Gail?"

I had to lie to him about how I felt. There was no sense in worrying him. "Everything's fine," I yelled back.

"You can't have many supplies. What are you eating?"

"I just had some chocolate." I didn't dare tell him how little I had eaten or that the chocolate had been the last of my food.

"Why don't you come down?" he asked. "You've proved your point. You've spent two nights in a tree. I never thought you'd do that. If you come down now, I could drive you to town. It would be a safe, easy way of getting out."

"Dad, I'm not giving up," I answered.

That was a stupid thing to say. I would have to give up very soon. But I might manage one more day. That was my goal.

He went quiet for a moment, crossing his arms on his chest. Then he added, "Gail, the guards let me through. I guess they hoped I might get you down. But I'm really not supposed to be here. Neddie Wakes told me to get lost. He said that Island Forest Products couldn't trust me anymore."

I leaned as far over the platform as I safely could. That way my father could see me a little better. I didn't want to put him through this. "Dad, I'm sorry about your job."

He threw up his arms. "No, I still have my job. It's just that they put me on vacation. Until further notice. Until we've cut down the forest, I guess."

He turned away. He always found it difficult to talk about his feelings. Then he looked up at me again.

"I was really angry when you climbed up there. It stopped the logging operation stone cold. It made me look bad. My own daughter on the other side. But that first night I kept worrying about you. Then you were there another night. I've tried calling you, but your phone's always turned off."

I groaned. I had turned off my phone to save the battery.

"Gail, if you come down now, I'm going to help you. We'll try to save Big Tree Country together."

I couldn't believe it. My father, the logger, made that offer. *Yes!* I felt like shouting to him. *I'll be right down.* Then I thought about Magic. Mr. Wakes and his men would cut the tree down as soon as I left. I looked around me at the great old tree. It looked so solid and comforting. It had stood for a thousand years. I had to do everything I could to save it.

My father called to me. "Gail, did you hear?"

I found it hard to answer him. At last, I did. "Dad, I can't do it. They'll cut down Magic."

"I thought you might say that." He folded his arms across his chest as if accepting that fact. He stayed quiet for a moment. Then he added, "You're having a big effect, you know. You've become a celebrity. I saw your photo on the front page of the city newspaper. As for TV, they've broadcast scenes of you in the tree again and again. There have been protests in front of Island Forest Products' office. Other people have been carrying signs in front of the government forestry building."

He shook his head as if in disbelief. Then he laughed a little again. "To think my daughter stirred all that up."

I felt something like pride when he told me that. My efforts to save Magic were achieving something. That idea helped me to forget how hungry and thirsty I felt for a few seconds. He turned to me again. "One more day, that's all you can do, Gail. Promise me you'll come down."

I didn't want him to worry. I lied again. "It's all right. I have some supplies left."

He shook his head. He probably didn't believe me. "If you need me, Gail, I'm only a phone call away." He turned to leave. "Don't wait too long. I want you safe."

I waved to my father and he left. As soon as he was gone, I was sorry that I hadn't left with him. I was hungry, thirsty, exhausted. The loggers seemed to be cutting down everything around me.

That evening, after the loggers stopped work, I drank the last of my water. I had no food left. I figured that I could stand one more night. Then I'd just have to give up. At least I had saved Magic for another day.

Chapter 6

Saved

The pain in my stomach woke me early Thursday morning. I would have gotten up except that I felt so weak. Holding my sides, I lay in the tree sit for an hour or two. I tried imagining that I was drinking a big bottle of water, or sinking my teeth into a juicy hamburger. My tongue seemed so thick and swollen. I could hardly lick my lips.

I felt too weak and thirsty to stay on Magic much longer. I even worried about my balance. If I didn't leave soon, I might not have the strength to get down.

I could hear the chainsaws. The loggers worked a little farther away now. But I knew that as soon as I left Magic, they would cut it down and every tree nearby.

At noon, I felt that I had to get down. I took my small pack. I put on the harness and slipped the rope through it. Then I climbed from the platform, slowly lowering myself down the rope.

Seven or eight meters above the ground, I looked down. I froze.

A young black bear, maybe three years old, was eating some green shoots at the base of Magic's trunk. The logging must have startled it from its hunting area on the other side of the road.

It frightened me a little to see a wild animal that size, but it also excited me. I had been trying to save the forest for animals like this one. So, I hung on the rope. I reached for my smart phone and took some photos. The bear didn't even look up. It just kept eating the plants, probably very happily. *Why are we so afraid of you?* I wondered. Although bears are much bigger than us, most of the time, they eat plants and berries, even grass. People eat a lot more meat and fish than bears do. Most of the time, bears eat insects like ants and bees.

The black bear looked almost like a very big dog with shiny black fur. It had a comical walk. It rolled from side to side as it walked through the undergrowth. Watching the black bear saddened me. Now the loggers would cut down the rest of the trees at Big Tree Country. This poor bear would have nowhere to go. Didn't he have a right to a home?

The bear rolled onto its back, scratching itself. Then it lay in the sun a while. The bear didn't seem to have a care in the world. I hung on my rope, watching.

Through the corner of my eye, I saw one of the security guards walking toward Magic. He held a gun. He must have seen the bear earlier and gone back to his tent for it.

I didn't know what to do. I'd seen a black bear shot once near my elementary school. The bear had been looking for food in the garbage bins near the building. A bear like that was dangerous around small children.

Now it seemed that I was watching that scene again. With horror, I saw the security guard raise the gun to his shoulder and point it at the bear. I held my breath. He lowered the gun again. He started moving closer, probably to get a better shot at the bear.

Back at my elementary school, our teacher had called the Forest Service and two men had arrived with guns. Our teacher stood with us, watching from behind a classroom window. The guns looked like the type that we saw on TV nature programs. The men smiled at us. We thought that they would put the bear to sleep and move him back to the wilderness. One of the men fired at the bear. It dropped to the ground, moaning with pain. The bear hadn't been put to sleep. It had been shot. The bear sounded like a person crying. Finally, the bear died. My teacher, my classmates, and I all started weeping.

It looked like that shooting was going to happen all over again. The guard stopped. He raised his rifle to shoot the bear.

I had to do something. I threw my pack at the bear. It crashed into the bushes. The bear ran just as the guard fired.

The guard shouted. "What are you doing? That bear's dangerous!"

He ran after the bear. But I knew he wouldn't catch him.

I called after him. "It's his forest. He deserves to *live*."

Somehow I found a hidden strength in my arms and legs. Quickly, I started climbing back up the tree. At last, I dragged myself onto the platform. I pulled up the rope after me so that when the guard returned, he couldn't climb it. Then I dropped onto the boards, drained.

But I had just saved a bear. I had more strength than I thought. I could hold out a little longer. Maybe an hour. Maybe all afternoon.

I lay there awhile, resting. To get my mind off thinking of food and water, I took out my phone and uploaded the photos of the bear onto my Facebook site. I wrote a message about saving the bear, too.

I noticed I had more than a thousand people commenting on my last post. Most of them urged me to keep fighting.

Someone had patched together a video clip of the protest three days ago and of me climbing Magic.

One look at my tangled hair on that climb and you'd say I'd been having a "bad hair" day. That video had drawn comments from around the world. A few people had even commented on my wild-looking hair. What an embarrassment. It looked like Shane's video. But he was in jail. I couldn't figure who could have put it up.

My smart phone rang. I sat up in surprise. The phone had an incoming message. I looked at the sender's name. But it was a new number. I read the text:

"We're in forest. Have supplies. Stay quiet. XX."

Help had come! There were people in the forest trying to get to me. They must have been afraid of being heard, so they had sent me a text.

I stared into the woods, trying to see if I could find them. Then I saw two figures by another big tree. They were setting up ropes and getting ready to climb. I tried to guess their plan. Maybe they were setting up another tree sit to expand the protest. It didn't make sense to me. And whatever their plan, they were much too close to my guards.

Sure enough, the two security guards noticed them and ran toward them. The climbers saw them coming. They dropped their supplies, and ran into the forest. The guards chased them. Soon the guards and the climbers disappeared.

So much for my rescue, I thought.

Then I noticed a slight movement in the undergrowth not far from Magic. I focused on that spot. Something moved a second time. Someone lay in the bushes. A person crawled very slowly, very carefully in the direction of Magic. A tall figure rose from the undergrowth. He wore a field green army jacket. He had on a green hat with some plants sticking out of it. He had painted his face with green and black jungle paint. But even in this fantastic disguise, Shane still wore his funny glasses, so I recognized him.

Shane had been texting me. He must have used a new phone to disguise his identity in case the message was discovered. But how had he gotten out of jail?

Then I heard my mother calling me. I hadn't noticed her at all. She suddenly appeared from some bushes right beside Magic.

She waved a small bag in the air. "Quick, send down the rope!" she called. "While the guards are chasing the climbers."

I dropped the rope and she clipped her bag onto it. Hurriedly, I pulled Mom's bag into the tree sit. Then I began emptying it onto the platform. Several water bottles. Some energy bars. Peanuts. Raisins. Dried apples. All sorts of treasures spilled out of it.

"I'm so glad we got through," she shouted to me. "I was desperate to get supplies to you."

I grabbed a water bottle and took a big drink from it. I ripped open an energy bar and stuffed it into my mouth. With my mouth full, I still managed to yell back, "This is like Christmas!"

Shane showed me a second bag. "If that was Christmas, then I've got your birthday present. Hurry up and drop the rope."

I threw him the rope. Then I pulled up his bag.

The second bag had cheese and bread, a solar-operated battery charger for my smart phone, a few warm clothes, and a raincoat. They had thought of everything.

I busied myself eating. I also asked them about the pack that I had thrown at the black bear. Shane found it near the base of the tree. So I sent down the rope and pulled it up.

It turned out that Shane and my mother had developed a complicated plan to get me supplies. They had tricked the security guards. The climbers I had seen earlier had been sent to distract the guards. They had led them away from Magic. That way Shane and my mother could get to me.

I had one big question for them. "How did you two get out of jail?"

Shane laughed. "You know all the jokes they make about lawyers? About my dad? It turns out, it is really good to have a lawyer in the family."

Mom started laughing, too. "We appeared in front of the judge. Shane's dad, the lawyer, was already there with a suitcase full of money to pay our bail."

Shane interrupted her, "Actually, it was only a briefcase."

My mother shrugged. "OK, a briefcase then. The main thing is, it had thousands of dollars in it."

Shane interrupted her again. "Ten thousand dollars, to be exact. The judge doesn't get to keep it. It's only bail money. For the moment, your mom and I are free. We're supposed to prepare our defense for the trial. So, we came to help you. But the judge warned us that if they catch us here again, they'll keep Dad's bail money."

"And they'll put us back in jail, too," my mother added.

That remark reminded us that the security guards might get back at any moment. We looked in the direction that the guards had run.

My mother must have thought of that, too. "We've got to go," she said.

Shane raised his hand. "Wait a minute. Gail, let me take your place."

"What do you mean?" I asked.

"Throw me the rope. I got you up there. And you've been through enough."

I leaned over the platform. "Shane, it was my choice. And you and Mom are on bail. You'll be in big trouble if they catch you here. And your dad would lose all his money."

Frustrated, Shane slapped the side of the tree. "I'm responsible for getting you into all this. I've got to do something!"

"You already have. You brought me supplies. You posted all those crazy things on the Internet."

My mother turned to us quickly. "The guards are coming!"

She and Shane ran toward the deepest and thickest part of the forest. The two guards hurried after them. But they were too slow to catch up to them, and soon I saw the guards return.

Chapter 7

The warning

Friday was the noisiest day yet. Not only were the loggers cutting down trees, but now Island Forest Products had brought in a crane. I caught glimpses of it through the trees as it lifted the fallen trees. Soon, they would be loaded onto trucks. I couldn't stand watching them destroy the forest.

By late afternoon, the loggers finished for the day, and I decided to climb higher up the tree, right to the top of Magic. I wanted to explore Magic and I thought I might be able to see more of the forest if I got higher up. I had to see how much of Big Tree Country had been cut down.

I tied one end of the climbing rope to my harness. If I lost my footing, I would not fall out of the tree. Even with the rope, I felt scared. I moved slowly. The tree trunk swayed a little as I climbed.

In the upper branches, I found a huge, empty bird's nest. The nest was about three meters high and two meters wide. It was made of twigs and moss, packed together with mud. It had to belong to the eagle I had seen earlier. Because our family had an eagle crest, I thought it might be a lucky sign. I tried not to disturb the nest as I climbed past it. I hadn't seen the eagle since the logging had begun, but I hoped that it would return. Eagles keep these nests for generations.

I climbed a little higher. I was still five or six meters from the top of the tree. I took another step. Suddenly, the whole upper tree swayed. I felt terrified. I grabbed some branches and clung to them. I stayed there for a few minutes, holding tight.

Then I relaxed a little. I had a safety rope so I wasn't going to fall. I leaned out from the tree a little. I looked out onto Big Tree Country.

The view almost broke my heart. On the south side of the road, a large bare patch had been cut out of the forest. It must have been as large as five or six city blocks. The loggers had not only cut down all of the trees, but they had also torn up all of the plants and undergrowth. All I could see was earth, rocks, and stumps. Nothing green had been left. I was looking at a wasteland.

I had to do something. I remembered that I had Ms. Wong's business card. So after I had climbed down to the tree sit, I called her office and left a message. I told her that I intended to stay in Magic until Big Tree Country became a park.

Saturday morning, it was quiet. For some reason, there were no loggers. Ms. Wong called me back. She informed me that our telephone call was being broadcast across the country on the news hour. She told her TV audience about Big Tree Country. Then she added, "Gail, we've been following your story all week. You've been living in a tree in the middle of a logging area."

She paused for dramatic effect. "Not only is that against the law, but it's a dangerous thing to do. Some people might even call it 'crazy.' What do you say, Gail?"

OK. I got it. That was her angle. The crazy girl in the tree.

I tried to keep my temper. "I'm not crazy. You just don't want to listen to me. I'm asking you to help save a forest."

Ms. Wong laughed nervously. "Sorry, I didn't mean to suggest you were crazy. We're listening to you, Gail."

"I wish people watching your program could see this forest. It's so old. It's so full of living things."

Ms. Wong cleared her throat. "I'm sure big trees mean a lot to you, Gail. But don't we need that timber to build houses and provide jobs? Those old trees are going to die sometime. They'll just be wasted if we don't cut them down first."

I struggled to control my feelings. I had to stay calm. "The old trees aren't dying. I'm living in a tree now that's over a thousand years old. It might live another two hundred years. That's not dying. Some of the birds living here can't survive anywhere else. And even when these old trees finally die, their trunks shelter animals, and help new trees to grow. Everything in this forest is connected."

"The government has an agreement with Island Forest Products," said Ms. Wong. "The only way the government can break that is by paying the company or offering them trees somewhere else."

"Then the government needs to do that. Big Tree Country is a national treasure. And I'm not leaving here until it's protected," I replied. "And I need help from everyone listening to this show. Please keep the pressure on the government."

"Are you sure you want to stay there, Gail?" asked Ms. Wong. "I've just been passed a note from the station weatherman. There's a big storm moving into your area."

"A storm?" I asked. That explained why it was so quiet. There hadn't been any loggers that day because of the storm.

"More like a hurricane," she warned. "We're talking about winds reaching a hundred kilometers an hour. It could be life-threatening in a tree."

I knew what I had to do. "I'm not leaving until we save Big Tree Country."

"Then stay safe, Gail," she urged. "We'll check in after the storm."

Chapter 8

Storm

High in Magic, I felt a slight wind on my face, blowing east. I could hear it passing through the trees. It sounded like a great sigh. The storm was coming all right.

A few hours later, gray storm clouds appeared overhead. They looked like battleships. The wind rattled the blue plastic sheet over the tree sit. I dug through my bags for the extra clothes that Shane and my mother had sent me. I hurriedly put them on and slipped my raincoat over the top.

I was going to call Shane, so I switched on my phone. It rang before I even punched in the number. But it was my father.

His voice crackled with static. The storm had started to interfere with my telephone line.

"Gail, there's a big storm coming. You've got to get out of there."

I held the phone to my ear as I crawled around the tree sit. I was searching through my supplies for a flashlight. "Dad, we've been through all this before."

His voice crackled again. "I tried to drive my truck up there. They turned me back at the gate. You've got to come down."

"I'm all right," I replied.

"I want you to know something. It's a good thing the company took me off this project. I was wrong about Big Tree Country. We need to save the forest. It isn't a lot to ask for."

I was shocked. "Dad, are you serious?"

"I already told you I'd help. Now I've got someone here who wants to talk to you."

He paused to pass the phone. I heard Mom's voice.

"Mom, where are you?" I asked.

"We're calling from my place. Your dad and I haven't agreed on much these past two years. But we've started talking again. And we agree on one big thing. You've got to get out of there."

Dad interrupted her. "Gail, you can get out with the security guards."

"I'd just get arrested. And what happens to the forest?"

"Don't worry about it. I'll tell you everything. The government's talking to Island Forest Products about a deal. Trading Big Tree Country for land somewhere else. The decision will be out any day now."

"Then I'd better stay here and keep the pressure on."

Mom started crying. "Gail, please . . ."

Hearing my mother cry was unbearable. I nearly started crying, too. That would have made it worse for my parents.

"Mom, Dad, sorry, I've got something to do here. I love you both. I'll call tomorrow."

I hung up the phone and switched it off. Was I making a mistake? Should I leave? Was staying worth the risk? A gust of wind flapped the plastic sheet. Some rain splashed onto my face. The storm was going to be a wet one. If the loggers weren't there, I didn't need to protect Magic. But there were still guards watching me.

Rain started falling. It fell faster and faster. Soon it streamed down. I looked out at the forest. I heard someone calling me. I leaned over the platform.

Neddie Wakes stood at the foot of Magic, wearing a heavy raincoat. He shouted, "We're pulling out our security team. We'll give you a ride back to town."

He had given me my last chance. Even my guards were leaving. I hesitated for a moment. Then I yelled back, "To the police station? No thanks."

He shook his finger at me. "You're making a big mistake." Then he ran off in the rain.

Even though I huddled under a plastic sheet, rain started splashing all over me. The wind grew stronger. It moaned like a ghost. I started thinking about the history I was studying at college. I often read about people making tough decisions. Making choices that risked everything. Now I knew how they felt.

Soon I heard branches in the tops of the trees crashing together. Slowly and very carefully, I moved to the edge of the platform and looked out. Within seconds, the rain soaked into my clothes. So much rain fell that I could see almost nothing; it seemed as though I was looking through a curtain. Shivering, I moved back under the plastic sheet and tried to warm up. Now I couldn't leave Magic if I tried. My fingers were too cold and wet to hold onto the rope. So, I dug through my pack and found some extra socks. I was wet, so I put on all the extra clothes I had.

Then the wind began to hammer against the tree. Branches from other trees cracked, tore off tree trunks, and whipped into the air. They hit other branches or slammed against tree trunks and fell to the forest floor. Among loggers, falling branches like that are called "widow makers." If I got down now, a falling branch might kill me.

Night fell and I still hadn't found a flashlight. I had put one somewhere, but I couldn't find it. In the darkness, the heavy rain and the roaring wind were even more terrifying. My only light was the display on my smart phone. I'd flash it now and then to lift my spirits.

I tried remembering my favorite songs. Most of them were love songs though. They just made me feel lonely and forgotten. So, I sat there, thinking of all the funny things that I had heard of or done in my life. Most of these times were jokes that Shane and I had played on people, and I smiled a little.

A screaming wind drove away these happy thoughts. *Now you've done it*, I thought to myself. *You played the heroine. Look what you've gotten yourself into.*

I needed to talk to someone, to hear them say that the storm would end, that I'd be all right. I didn't dare call my parents. They were already sick with worry. I thought of Shane. I reached for my phone. My fingers felt frozen. I could hardly punch in his number. I waited. Nothing. I tried it again. Then I listened to the phone. It had no dial tone. The storm had knocked out my telephone connection.

Then a huge gust blew right into the tree sit. It flipped me into the air. Screaming, I dropped onto the boards with a thump. It felt as though I had just fallen off a bicycle. Though bruised and aching, I sat right up and grabbed hold of the nearest tree branch. I held it with all my strength. My life seemed to depend on it. Tears came to my eyes. I clenched my teeth.

My hands formed into fists. My whole body tensed with the effort. But I knew I could never keep that hold all night. I was going to die. I closed my eyes.

In that moment, I spoke to Magic. It was something like a prayer. *I have to get through the night. Help me do that. Then I can save the forest.* Then an idea came to me. I remembered how trees behave in storms. Trees bend with the wind. They never fight it. So, I realized that I had to bend with the wind, too. I relaxed my grip on the tree branch. Then I let it go. But I also put on the rope harness and tied myself to the tree branch. Then I let the wind blow me about the platform. It tossed me right then left. I shouted and rolled with it. I screamed as it howled. I sang as it whipped by me. And each time the wind took me, I just let go. I surrendered to it.

The punishment lasted for hours. Finally, I was too exhausted to even bend with the wind. I just had to rest. I was so tired that I began drifting off to sleep. In those last few minutes, I wondered if I would ever wake up.

Chapter 9

The good news

A puzzling bright blue light appeared. Was I dead?

Then I heard the crackle of plastic. I was staring at the blue plastic sheet hanging over the tree sit. It was Sunday morning. Shakily, I stood up. My clothes felt damp. But the rain had stopped.

I breathed in a wonderful fresh smell. It was damp and smelled of the earth, the smell of a forest after a rainfall. I found a plastic container stuck in Magic's branches. It was filled with water. I raised the rain water to my lips and drank some. Delicious—the freshest water you could drink. I sat down by my food bag and ate some nuts and raisins. I found some cheese, too, and ate that.

I noticed that I had a neighbor. A squirrel with soft, silky gray fur and a big bushy tail sat on the edge of the tree sit. I tossed it a few nuts. The squirrel took them and hurried up a tree branch. Squeaking at me, it sat there eating the nuts.

I laughed. "I guess you're hungry, too."

I checked my phone. The line remained down. I had no way of contacting anyone to find out news about the storm.

I did the next best thing. I started climbing up Magic to take a look. I took the same precaution as before and tied myself onto a safety rope. The trunk was wet. I had to be very careful. I moved slowly. I reminded myself that I had plenty of time.

As I climbed higher in Magic, I passed the eagle's nest. It was empty as before. The cloudy sky overhead looked like a ragged white sheet. Pieces of blue shone through it. The weather seemed to be getting warm again.

I got as high in the tree as I dared. Then I looked down. Nothing had been cut down in the forest since I'd looked on Friday. But the storm had struck the logging road. Broken tree branches and even a few small trees lay scattered across it. That would slow down any loggers returning to Big Tree Country.

I started down the tree. When I got to the eagle's nest again, I noticed a long brown feather sticking out of it. Maybe the eagle had ridden out the storm with me. Eagle feathers have always been sacred to native people, sometimes given to warriors for bravery. I strained to reach it. I had stood up to a logging company and I had stayed in Magic during the storm. I just managed to pick the eagle feather up. I tied it onto one of my braids.

The storm was over and I was alive and the loggers were gone. I felt so happy that I wanted to climb down Magic and run through the forest. I had grown tired of living in a tree. But I also had repairs to make to the tree sit. The blue plastic sheet had been torn in places. And some of my clothes were wet. So I repaired the sheet, and I hung my wet clothes to dry on some branches.

Now that the loggers were gone, the natural rhythms of the forest began to reappear. I could hear birds in the trees again. I thought about the black bear I had chased away. Maybe he would come back, too. Of course, I hoped that the eagle would return to its nest in Magic. And I decided to stay in Magic one more day. That would make it a whole week that I'd lived in a tree.

On Monday morning, there was still no sign of any loggers. I sat in Magic just listening to the forest. In a few hours, my anniversary would pass. A whole week spent living in a tree.

By the afternoon, the week had passed. But I still couldn't decide when to climb down Magic. And it could only be a break. The loggers were going to come back. And they would likely return soon.

Then I saw Shane walking in the forest. Surprised, I shouted to him, "What are you doing here?"

He ran over to the tree and yelled to me, "Gail, you're all right! I kept trying to call you. The lines were knocked down."

"You walked here?" I leaned over the platform. "It must have taken you hours."

"You can say that again. I started at about sunrise and followed the road. I kept hoping someone would call in a helicopter rescue for you. They could have picked me up on the way. That would have been great! And a lot easier than hiking, too. But emergency services are too busy. We've got flooding in town. Smashed cars. Downed power lines. Fishermen in sinking boats. It's a total disaster."

"Wait a minute. How did you get past the gate on the road?" I asked.

Shane laughed. "There's no one there now. I doubt there ever will be again."

"What do you mean?"

Shane didn't say a word. He just stood there, grinning, with his arms folded on his chest.

"What are you grinning about?"

"Have I got news!" He added, breathlessly, "The government decided. Big Tree Country is going to be a park."

I shook my head. "I don't believe it. Where did you hear this?"

"I got the news from your father, *the logger*. He's had a complete change of heart. He'd just heard it from one of his contacts. The government must have decided late Friday. Maybe Saturday."

"Let me get this right. Dad told you that?" I asked.

"His change of heart had a lot to do with you," replied Shane. "He told me that. You stood up for your ideals. That reminded him how he used to feel about things. Now he's a changed man. And he's driving up here with your mom today. They're desperate to see you. They've been worried sick. He even contacted Ann Wong at *The Nightly News*. She's coming over to get the big story about the new park."

The news about Big Tree Country began to sink in. After all of our sacrifices. The blockade. The people willing to go to jail. My week spent in Magic. The big storm. Now it had all proved worthwhile. "We've really done it, then. We've saved Big Tree Country."

"You mean *you've* done it, Gail. You're practically a front-page story these days. You're all over the Internet."

I groaned when I heard that. "Shane, we have to do something about that video."

Shane started laughing. "You mean the 'bad hair' video? The one where your hair looks like a broom?"

"Thanks a lot," I replied.

He laughed even harder. "Just forget it. That video's been re-posted by so many people, in so many places, you'll never get it off the Internet. You'll just have to start a new fashion."

"It's all your fault, Shane Barnett." I tried to sound annoyed. But I couldn't help laughing, too. I felt so happy. After everything we had been through, we'd saved Big Tree Country.

Shane waved. "Come on down."

"I can hardly wait," I answered. "Give me a few minutes to put my things together."

I started throwing clothes into my bag, then my water bottle and the rest of my food. I had thought that I'd be so happy to leave Magic. Because of the security guards, I'd been almost a prisoner. I was desperate to have a shower and I looked forward to sleeping in my bed. But now I felt a little depressed. I had spent a week living in a huge fir tree. And I'd been doing everything I could think of to save it. Those were experiences that few people ever had. Now that time was over.

I stood on the platform and looked at the branches that stretched so far above me. I patted the rough bark of this thousand-year-old tree. Magic had protected me during the storm. With both arms, I reached around Magic's trunk and held it tightly. I felt glad to be alone. I didn't have to explain my feelings to anyone.

Then I put on my harness, attached the rope, and lowered myself down the tree.

Once I was on the ground, Shane came over and we hugged each other. We had both been through so much. We held each other for a few seconds.

Then I thought about how dirty and sweaty I must be. I hadn't washed my hair in days. And it just seemed too awkward to be in each other's arms. We had always just been friends. I felt embarrassed. I guess Shane did, too. We both dropped our arms.

At first, my voice choked with emotion. Then I managed to thank him for coming for me.

Shane had problems speaking, too. He cleared his throat a few times. Then he joked a little. "Getting here was just a walk in the park."

"A really big park," I said, teasing him.

"And a really long walk," he added.

He was the same old Shane. And I couldn't ask for a better friend.

We might have stayed there awhile making light conversation. But we heard voices. People were approaching Magic. I recognized one of them, and a chill went up my spine.

Chapter 10

Magic is attacked

Neddie Wakes stood there in his Island Forest Products' hardhat. With him were four loggers in their hardhats, carrying chainsaws.

"How did you get here?" asked Shane.

Mr. Wakes gestured toward his crew. "It's amazing what a few good men can do. We cleared the road with our chainsaws. Then we drove up."

I felt outraged. "This is a park now."

Mr. Wakes gave me an evil-looking smile. "The idea of making this a park really bothers me. All this fine wood wasted. So we're going to do something about that."

He gave a nod to one of the loggers. The man started his chainsaw. It roared into life.

"You can't cut down trees in a park. It's against the law," Shane protested.

Mr. Wakes shrugged. "The government still has to announce the park officially. So, we'll say we never knew about it. That's why we were still logging the old trees. And the first one we're cutting down is your favorite."

I shook my head. "You can't do that. Not after all this."

"Just watch me." He laughed. "A big tree like this is probably worth $20,000. Besides, your tree's become a symbol. A symbol for preserving old forests. That's the kind of symbol I don't like."

I stepped in front of Magic. "I'm not letting you."

Shane moved to my side. "Me neither."

Mr. Wakes turned to his men. "Get them out of the way."

One man grabbed me and pulled me away. He twisted my right arm behind me and held me back from the tree.

The logger with the chainsaw put it down. He and the other two men closed in on Shane. Shane tried swinging at them with his fists. But he couldn't keep them off. They were punching him from different directions. One of them hit hard in the stomach. Shane bent over with pain. The other two loggers pinned his arms back. The first man came in and hit him in the face.

I struggled to get free. "You're hurting him!"

Mr. Wakes raised a hand to stop them. "Don't overdo it. Just hang onto them while we cut down the tree."

There was a shout from the forest. "I think you'd better let them go."

We all turned in surprise. Then my father walked into view.

Mr. Wakes stared at him. "What are you doing here? You're on leave."

Dad folded his arms across his chest. "I'm here to enjoy the new park. Thanks for clearing the road for me."

Mr. Wakes shook his fist at him. "You're fired, Mr. Klutesi."

"No, you can't fire me. I'm quitting." Dad turned to the man holding me. He was someone my father knew. "I'd let my daughter go if I were you, Jack."

The man holding my arms relaxed his grip. I pulled free of him.

Dad turned to the men holding Shane. "I'd ease up on him, too, if I were you guys. You know his father's one of the best lawyers around. After he takes you to court, you'd be lucky if you still own the shirt on your back."

Shane was released. The three men moved quickly away.

"What are you doing?" shouted Mr. Wakes. "They're not supposed to be here. We built the road. We have the right to cut down the trees in this forest."

"You mean you had the right. This is a park now," Dad replied.

Mr. Wakes grew so angry, he was almost screaming. "It's not a park yet! It hasn't been announced."

My father replied very calmly. "Not yet, maybe. But the government has a signed agreement with Island Forest Products. So, you're not supposed to be here cutting down trees."

The loggers looked back and forth at the argument between my father and Mr. Wakes. Mr. Wakes was their boss. But Dad had been their supervisor. They didn't know what to do.

Dad walked around the men. "Are you guys actually getting paid today? I doubt it since logging here is now illegal. The company won't want any records. And if it's illegal, you're not going to get paid and you might get arrested." He pointed his finger at Mr. Wakes. "And I don't think cutting down Magic is going to look very good on national TV."

"What are you talking about?" asked Mr. Wakes.

Dad gestured behind him. My mother was leading Ms. Wong and her cameraman into the forest. They waved to us.

"I promised Ms. Wong a news story today," Dad explained. "I thought I was going to be breaking the story about the new park. But just think of the bad publicity for Island Forest Products if everyone watching *The Nightly News* sees you cutting down the most famous tree in the country."

Mr. Wakes threw up his arms. "All right, all right, you win! But don't you ever come looking for a job at Island Forest Products."

Dad laughed. "Believe me, I never will."

Swearing, and at times shaking his head, Mr. Wakes gathered his crew together. None of them looked at us. They just picked up their chainsaws and headed for their trucks.

Ms. Wong held up her hand to stop them. "Wait a minute. Now that you've lost Big Tree Country, we want to hear your side of the story."

She and her cameraman started following after them. She turned back to us for a moment. "We'll be back later for your story!"

Chapter 11

Forest forever

Mom had brought a first aid kit, so she looked Shane over. She examined the bruises on his face and his split lip. "How do you feel?" she asked.

He rubbed his face, but he smiled. "It still hurts. But I don't think I've ever been happier. We've saved Big Tree Country."

My father patted him on the back. "You're all right, Shane. They can't keep a good man down."

I turned to my father. "You saved Magic. What happened, Dad? Are you an ecologist now?"

"No, I'll always be a logger. But even a logger can see that some places are worth saving. And you've taught me something, too, Gail."

"What do you mean?" I asked.

Dad smiled. "I'd forgotten how to stand up for anything. Sometimes when you get older, you get too busy trying to make a living." He looked up at Magic. "I'd always loved the outdoors. That was why I wanted to work in forests in the first place. Now I realize that I should be working harder to protect them."

He looked at Shane. "Don't worry about breaking your bail agreement. I don't think anyone's going to report you. Island Forest Products won't want people to know what Mr. Wakes was trying to do here."

"You can say that again," replied Shane.

My father continued. "There's something else I've been thinking about. I wonder if the new park agreement should include us, too. What about the Nuu-chah-nulth claim to this land?"

"Maybe your people could be in charge of the park," Shane suggested.

Dad nodded. "I guess the government will have to do some talking with us."

He looked back at me. He stroked his chin thoughtfully. "Gail, we'll have to take you to the police station, I'm afraid. But now there's an agreement on a park here, I don't think a judge will punish you that heavily. Maybe there'll be a fine and some community volunteer work."

I hugged him. "Dad, thanks for everything."

Mom had been standing a little ways off. "I'm pretty impressed with your father, too."

Dad moved toward her. "Does that mean we're getting together again?"

She put her hands on her waist. "I'd like that. But let's start as friends and see where that takes us."

He offered to shake her hand. "All right, I'd like to be your friend."

Mom took his arm and put it around her shoulder. We stood together for a moment in my father's arms. Then she slipped out from under his arm.

"Wait, I have something for you," she told me.

She took off the pack she had been carrying. Then she reached inside and took out her button blanket. She held it up and I could see the eagle.

"This is yours now." She placed it over my shoulders and tied it on.

"Are you sure?" I asked.

There were tears in her eyes. She put her arms around me. "Your great-grandmother would be so proud of you."

Dad wrapped the three of us in his big arms again. We all hugged.

I looked at Shane, worried that he might feel left out. But he smiled and waved to me.

Then I looked up at Magic. The giant fir tree stood in Big Tree Country as it had for hundreds of years. Magic would continue to grow and spread its branches farther into the sky. I saw an eagle circling the tree and I touched the eagle feather in my braid. Now I felt certain that the great bird would return to its nest in the tree. Now that we had our park, there would be a forest there forever.

Review: Chapters 1–4

A. Match the characters in the story to their descriptions.

Ann Wong	Bob Klutesi	Gail Klutesi	Officer Savard
Grace Klutesi	Neddie Wakes	Shane Barnett	

1. _____ often works with a cameraman.

2. _____ calls the police to break up the protest.

3. _____ narrates the story.

4. _____ gets accused of losing past ideals.

5. _____ is the best climber in the story.

6. _____ owns a beautiful button blanket.

7. _____ sees Gail pulling up the climbing rope.

B. Read each statement and circle whether it is true (T) or false (F).

1. The button blanket has a whale design on it.   T / F
2. Island Forest Products has the right to cut down the trees.   T / F
3. Gail studies history at her university.   T / F
4. Shane organized the protest on the logging road.   T / F
5. The TV reporter has followed the story for two years.   T / F
6. Gail believes that Magic is 800 years old.   T / F
7. Bob's chief argument for logging is that it provides work.   T / F
8. Shane's father is a wealthy lawyer in Johnson Bay.   T / F
9. Two policemen came to break up the protest.   T / F
10. Shane left his climbing harness on the road.   T / F

C. Choose the best answer for each question.

1. Gail tells Ann that the government should make Big Tree Country a park because it _____.

   a. is something that everyone wants

   b. will attract many tourists

   c. will create more jobs than logging

   d. will protect some very big old trees

2. Shane criticizes the company's plans to cut down the forest because _____.

   a. the company will not replant any trees

   b. the people in the town will not be hired

   c. the forest will take a long time to grow back

   d. the work is too dangerous for Bob's men

3. Shane got the idea to make a rope climbing harness from _____.

   a. a book that he read

   b. a class that he took

   c. a friend of his

   d. a video on the Internet

4. In the story that Gail remembers about the bear village, the bears _____.

   a. fight with people over land ownership

   b. capture her after she makes fun of them

   c. fear people and often run away from them

   d. reject children who are part human, part bear

Review: Chapters 5–8

A. Number these events in the order that they happened (1–6).

a. Gail receives a secret message promising supplies. _____

b. Gail saves a black bear from being killed. _____

c. Gail's parents beg her to leave Magic because of a storm. _____

d. The loggers start cutting down trees very close to Magic. _____

e. Bob secretly visits Gail to convince her to come down. _____

f. Neddie Wakes and his security guards surround the tree. _____

B. Complete the summary with words from the box.

a warning	an agreement	connection	rescue
a message	help	bail	supplies

Gail Klutesi posts **1.** _____ on Facebook about saving the
black bear. She reads a text from someone promising **2.** _____ .
Shane and Grace have been released from jail because his father pays for
3. _____ . They bring Gail clothes and other **4.** _____ .
Ann reminds Gail that Island Forest Products and the government have
5. _____ . Several people give Gail **6.** _____
about the storm. Her father tries to **7.** _____ her, but when he
drives up the road, he is stopped at the gate. The storm knocks out Gail's
phone **8.** _____ .

C. Complete the crossword puzzle using the clues below.

Across

5. Ann's TV news program has a large _____ .

6. Ann Wong suggests that Gail might be _____ .

7. As a result of all the coverage on TV and in newspapers, Gail becomes a/an _____ .

9. Neddie offers Gail a/an _____ if she will come down from the tree.

11. Magic is almost hit by a falling _____ .

Down

1. Shane wears a/an _____ when he comes to the forest.

2. Shane and Grace had to appear before a/an _____ .

3. During the storm, Gail ties herself to a/an _____ .

4. Bob Klutesi is forced to go on _____ for a while.

8. The noise of the logging scares away a/an _____ living in Magic.

9. A bear was _____ at Gail's elementary school.

10. Bob reveals that the company and the government may make a/an _____ .

Review: Chapters 9–11

A. Answer the questions using the correct names.

1. Who is the first to see Gail after the storm? _____

2. Who rescues Gail and Shane from the loggers? _____

3. Who is Gail's mother leading into the forest? _____

4. Who teaches Bob Klutesi how to stand up for ideals? _____

5. Who gives away a button blanket? _____

B. Choose the best answer for each question.

1. For Gail, the eagle feather represents _____ .

   a. a special tribe

   b. her bravery

   c. rare animals

2. Shane gets past the gate at the entrance to the road because _____ .

   a. he ran past the guard

   b. no one is at the gate

   c. the guard didn't see him

3. Neddie's excuse for cutting down Magic is that _____ .

   a. the government hasn't announced the park yet

   b. there is no law against doing this

   c. no one will dare complain against him

4. Bob's unanswered question at the end is about _____ .

   a. his future with Island Forest Products

   b. Grace becoming a friend

   c. the Nuu-chah-nulth land claim

Answer Key

Chapters 1–4

A:
1. Ann Wong; **2.** Neddie Wakes; **3.** Gail Klutesi; **4.** Bob Klutesi; **5.** Shane Barnett;
6. Grace Klutesi; **7.** Office Savard

B:
1. F; **2.** T; **3.** T; **4.** F; **5.** F; **6.** F; **7.** T; **8.** T; **9.** F; **10.** T

C:
1. d; **2.** c; **3.** b; **4.** d

Chapters 5–8

A:
5, 4, 6, 2, 3, 1

B:
1. a message; **2.** help; **3.** bail; **4.** supplies; **5.** an agreement; **6.** a warning;
7. rescue; **8.** connection

C:
Across:
5. audience; **6.** crazy; **7.** celebrity; **9.** sandwich; **11.** tree

Down:
1. disguise; **2.** judge; **3.** branch; **4.** vacation; **8.** eagle; **9.** shot; **10.** deal

Chapters 9–11

A:
1. Shane Barnett; **2.** Bob Klutesi; **3.** Ann Wong (and her cameraman);
4. Gail Klutesi; **5.** Grace Klutesi

B:
1. b; **2.** b; **3.** a; **4.** c

Background Reading:

Spotlight on . . . *Old growth forests*

Sizeable old growth forests can be found along the northwest coast of the USA and the west coast of Canada. These unique environments provide a home to many plants and animals, but not many have been preserved in parks. Mice, squirrels, and similar animals eat the fir tree seeds. Black bears live in the forest, fishing in the clean streams. Tall old growth trees provide bald eagles with nesting places. The marbled murrelet, a rare bird, tends to nest in moss that grows on trees about 175 to 250 years old. Some Douglas fir trees in these forests are over 1,000 years old and have reached heights of 120 meters.

For thousands of years, different aboriginal or "First Nations" peoples also made their homes in these coastal forests. They used small numbers of the trees to make their homes and boats. They also created totems from the trees, making large carved poles with images of animals and people to decorate their homes.

About 150 years ago, large numbers of settlers from eastern Canada and the USA started moving to the northwest coast. They cut down the trees to build homes and ships, and to export the wood to countries around the world.

Today, logging companies are cutting down the last old growth forests. They replant the forests after they have logged them. However, the trees in these "second growth" forests are only allowed to grow to 40 to 60 years of age before they are harvested. As a result, the habitat for the plants and animals in these forests has been damaged.

Protests of Logging Old Growth Forests

In recent years, there have been many conflicts between logging companies and the environmental groups and First Nations people who wish to protect the remaining old growth forests. In British Columbia, the setting of this story, these conflicts include Meares Island (1984), South Moresby (1987),

and Clayoquot Sound (1993), when over 800 people were arrested and many put on trial. First of all, the groups opposed to logging tried to educate the public about the problem. Then they blocked roads to slow down the logging. As a last resort, some protestors built tree sits and lived in them, risking their lives to save the trees. In each conflict, a settlement was reached, preserving large areas of the forests.

The best-known tree sit was by Julia Butterfly Hill who lived in "Luna," a 54-meter-tall California redwood tree between 600 to 1,000 years old. She stayed in Luna for two years between December 10, 1997 and December 18, 1999. At the end of her struggle, she saved Luna and a large part of an ancient forest. She wrote an award-winning book about her experiences, called *The Legacy of Luna: The Story of a Tree, a Woman, and the Struggle to Save the Redwoods.*

Think About It

1. What are some natural areas that you know about or that exist where you live? What dangers do they face?
2. How do you think we should manage the conflict between developing our resources and preserving them?

Glossary

bail   (*n.*)   money given in exchange for releasing an arrested person so that he or she can prepare for trial

bark   (*n.*)   the outside skin of a tree trunk

braids   (*n.*)   long hair woven into narrow bands

chainsaw   (*n.*)   a gas-powered saw with a chain of quickly revolving metal teeth used to cut trees

claws   (*n.*)   the pointed horny nails of an animal's or bird's feet

handcuffs   (*n.*)   a metal or plastic device to chain a person's hands together in order to capture them

hardhat   (*n.*)   a worker's safety helmet made of hard plastic

harness   (*n.*)   equipment fitting around the waist that can be attached to a rope for safety in climbing

logger   (*n.*)   a person who cuts down trees, turning them into logs that can be processed into wood products

shrug   (*n.*)   a gesture made by lifting and dropping the shoulders that means a person does not know something

squirrel   (*n.*)   a medium-sized rodent with a bushy tail, often gray in color, that lives in trees

stump   (*n.*)   the small part of a tree that remains in the ground attached to the roots after a tree has been cut down

trunk   (*n.*)   the main part of a tree that supports the branches and is attached to the roots